YOUR KNOWLEDGE HAS VALUE

AF131295

- We will publish your bachelor's and master's thesis, essays and papers

- Your own eBook and book - sold worldwide in all relevant shops

- Earn money with each sale

Upload your text at www.GRIN.com and publish for free

Mark Schauer

Abuses and Allotments. The setting of Louise Erdrich's "Tracks" and its importance

GRIN Verlag

Bibliografische Information der Deutschen Nationalbibliothek:

Die Deutsche Bibliothek verzeichnet diese Publikation in der Deutschen National-
bibliografie; detaillierte bibliografische Daten sind im Internet über http://dnb.d-
nb.de/ abrufbar.

Imprint:

Copyright © 2011 GRIN Verlag GmbH
Druck und Bindung: Books on Demand GmbH, Norderstedt Germany
ISBN: 978-3-656-46698-7

This book at GRIN:

http://www.grin.com/en/e-book/230263/abuses-and-allotments-the-setting-of-
louise-erdrich-s-tracks-and-its

GRIN - Your knowledge has value

Der GRIN Verlag publiziert seit 1998 wissenschaftliche Arbeiten von Studenten, Hochschullehrern und anderen Akademikern als eBook und gedrucktes Buch. Die Verlagswebsite www.grin.com ist die ideale Plattform zur Veröffentlichung von Hausarbeiten, Abschlussarbeiten, wissenschaftlichen Aufsätzen, Dissertationen und Fachbüchern.

Visit us on the internet:

http://www.grin.com/

http://www.facebook.com/grincom

http://www.twitter.com/grin_com

Abuses and Allotments: The setting of Louise Erdrich's *Tracks* and its importance

by Mark Schauer

The story of Native American history since contact with Europeans has been
one of land and the diametrically opposed conception of it held by both groups: the
former saw it as a setting that supplied sustenance and belonged to everyone within
a tribal range, while the latter conceived of it as a commodity that could be owned,
parceled, and sold by individuals. Though they lacked the insatiable greed of their
colonizers, the importance of land was keenly felt by those who had lived on it for
generations. In Louise Erdrich's *Tracks*, the character Nanapush states the dilemma
thusly: "Land is the only thing that lasts life to life. Money burns like tinder, flows off
like water. And as for government promises, the wind is steadier" (*T* 33). Over the
course of centuries, the colonizers' sustained assault against indigenous people
resulted in, "the Native cultures (being) disposed, nearly wiped out by 1900 (Lincoln
7). Having seized most of the continent, the colonizers were not content to merely
confine what was left of the decimated first inhabitants on reservations and leave
them to live as best they could using traditional means. Instead, the dominant power
structure wanted to 'assimilate' the indigenous population by dividing what was left of
native land and parceling it out in individual acreages. *Tracks* is, "in part an autopsy
of this process, whereby place becomes property," and thus is deeply and inherently
political (Larson 1). "As a Native American writer, Erdrich has to deal with the fact
that Native Americans have been constantly underrepresented or misrepresented in
traditional Western historical narratives. By simply writing about Native American
history and peoples, she counters the invisibility of minority life and history in
American mainstream society" (Quennet 145). For the full effect of this necessary
reclaiming of Native history, however, the *place* in which the historical fiction is set is
of vital importance. Erdrich herself has opined that, "a traditional storyteller fixes
listeners in an unchanging landscape combined of myth and reality" (Erdrich 1). The
preponderance of evidence shows that in *Tracks*, as well as its chronological
sequels *Love Medicine, The Beet Queen,* and *The Bingo Palace,* this landscape is in
North Dakota in locales that strongly resemble the Turtle Mountain Reservation in

the north central part of the state and Erdrich's hometown of Wahpeton, in the southeast on the Minnesota border.

Nonetheless, much has been made of the similarity of the fate of the Ojibwe characters in *Tracks* with the historical outrage perpetrated against the White Earth Anishinaabeg from the signing of the Dawes Act in 1887 to the nadir of Native American wellbeing in the early 1920s. Eager to assimilate indigenous people into the dominant society in the wake of the American Civil War, the timber-rich White Earth Reservation was envisioned by white policymakers as a showcase for the effort to convert communal, nomadic natives into yeoman farmers tending allotments as small-time capitalists. The objective solidified twenty years later in the General Allotment (Dawes) Act of 1887, in which tribal members across the nation were eligible to receive up to 160 acres of land exempt from, "sale or alienation for twenty-five years" (Meyer 391). (*Tracks* begins in 1912, 25 years after the Dawes Act.) Surplus land remaining after these allotments were issued was opened for white settlement, which immediately led to a net loss of more than 65% of Native-controlled land (Larson 6). Not satisfied with this massive infusion of land onto the market, however, in the first decade of the twentieth century Minnesota congressmen Moses Clapp and Halvor Steenerson, acting on behalf of timber interests hungry for White Earth land, sponsored bills that first allowed mixed-blood tribal members to sell timber rights, followed by a 1906 act that removed all restrictions from land sales on White Earth and other reservations. Massive allotment fraud, unscrupulous tactics by land speculators, a pseudo-scientific attempt to prove that virtually all of the tribal members were mixed-bloods and thus not legally eligible for allotments, and aggressive tax delinquency seizures resulted in 99% of the reservation being taken from tribal members by 1920. In 1988, the same year *Tracks* was published, Erdrich co-wrote with her then-husband Michael Dorris an expose of this travesty that was published in *The New York Times Magazine*, which added to speculation that the politicized novel was a thinly veiled account of White Earth. This connection was particularly emphasized by respected critic James Stripes in his "The Problem(s) of (Anishinaabe) History in the Fiction of Louise Erdrich: Voices and Contexts", which was more noted for pointing out the connection between trees, lumbering, and the triplicate government documents Nanapush so derides, but also strongly implied that the story is set on the White Earth Reservation.

2

Lost in the rush to place *Tracks* in Minnesota, however, was the fact that the historical Turtle Mountain Ojibwe in North Dakota experienced just as egregious a theft of timber-rich tribal land, both prior and subsequent to the Dawes Act. Critic P. Jane Hafen points out that, "although the particularities are consistent with the history at the White Earth Chippewa Reservation, the scenario could have and has happened dozens of places" (Hafen 326). The Turtle Mountain Reservation was one of those places, and in some ways served as the textbook example for the fraud committed at White Earth. In fact, were it not for the sustained political struggle waged by tribal leaders, the Turtle Mountain band may actually have been forced to relocate to White Earth prior to the time period of *Tracks*.

Traditionally, the Turtle Mountain band ranged across 10 million acres in the north-central part of North Dakota, and tribal chief Little Shell advocated forcefully for federal recognition of this claim. In 1882, President Chester Arthur signed an executive order creating a reservation that was a small fraction of this size. Nonetheless, Nanapush, who had seen "fifty winters" in 1912 and was thus 20 years old at the time the reservation was codified, recalled these days to Lulu as ones in which, "it would have taken four days to walk the length of this reservation" (*T* 191). "At the time, the reservation was twenty townships in size": but within three months, Congress appropriated money to remove the Turtle Mountain Chippewa to the White Earth Reservation in an effort to reduce costs through consolidation of Indian agents, and white settlers desirous of even more of the prime farm and timber land in the Turtle Mountains contended that most of the Turtle Mountain Chippewa were in fact mixed-blood Canadians (Camp 21). President Arthur responded by expelling hundreds of Ojibwe from the tribal rolls and cutting twenty townships out of the reservation, leaving a tiny postage stamp of land for the band (Camp 24). These newly contracted boundaries made the reservation far smaller than its White Earth counterpart, and the same feint of supposed ineligibility of mixed blood tribal members was used against the Anishinaabeg in Minnesota some twenty years later, only with the added wrinkle of racist pseudo-science to 'prove' the denials were legitimate. (For example, "real Indians were supposed to have skin so tough that a scratch would leave no mark" (Erdrich-Dorris).)Efforts to remove the Turtle Mountain band to White Earth continued even after the Dawes Act, however, despite the continuing political efforts of leaders like Little Shell. Eventually, in 1892, three years after North Dakota became a state, the government's McCumber Commission made a settlement with a council of mixed bloods not affiliated with Little Shell: the agreement solidified the smallest boundaries of the reservation, prohibited the reinstatement of alleged Canadian mixed bloods who had been expelled from the tribal rolls, and called for a $1 million payment in exchange for forfeiture of all Ojibwe claims on the 10 million acres taken from them (Camp 28). The paltry ten cents per acre offered was dwarfed by previous settlements of as much as $2.50 per acre made to other tribes. (Camp 28) Though encroachment by white settlers continued unabated, the tribe did not capitulate until 1904, four years after Little Shells' death, and evidently Nanapush played a role in this delay: "As a young man, I had made my reputation as a government interpreter, that is, until the Beauchamp Treaty signing, in which I said to Rift-In-A-Cloud, 'Don't put your thumb in the ink.' One of the officials understood and I lost my job" (T 100).

The Burke Act of 1904 coincided with the settlement, but by this time, the Turtle Mountain Reservation was not large enough to grant 160 acre claims to every enrolled member of the tribe. Consequently, "the majority of the allotments were made on the public domain, some of them as distant as Montana and South Dakota. A substantial number of Turtle Mountain people were assigned land in western North Dakota, while others took allotments at Graham Island, near Devils Lake" (Camp 30). Indeed, according to the Census Bureau the modern-day Turtle Mountain Reservation has land holdings in parts of 22 counties across the Dakotas and Montana. "Tragically, had the reservation been kept at its original 1882 size, the need for public domain allotments would have been minimal" (Camp 30). The forced diaspora of various characters mentioned in Tracks strongly suggest that they are members of the Turtle Mountain band, not the White Earth Anishinaabeg . In Chapter Two, Pauline reports that her Aunt Regina's husband Dutch, "never did adopt her son, Russell, whose father lived somewhere in Montana now" (T 13). Perceptive critics have also identified traces of the diaspora in the novel: "Margaret Kashpaw has been granted an allotment on what was once Ojibwa reservation land, but all of her older children have had to move to Montana, the site of their allotments" (Stookey 72). Regardless of the location of the allotments, however, the same legal devices used to swindle the native land holders at White Earth had taken their toll on the Turtle Mountain Ojibwe. "By 1920, the Turtle Mountain agency rolls showed a full-blood population of 166: of these, 112 already had their land in either restricted fee patent status or full fee patent status" (Camp 35). Near the end of *Tracks,* in 1919, the novel's principle characters are about to lose their land to tax delinquency, and while recovering from starvation with government rations brought by the priest, pour over a map of the reservation:

> "…we examined the lines and circles of the homesteads paid up—Morissey, Pukwan, Hat, Lazzarres everywhere. They were colored green. The lands that were gone out of the tribe- to deaths with no heirs, to sales, to the lumber company—were painted a pale and rotten pink. Those in question, a sharper yellow. At the center of a bright square was Matchimanito, a small blue triangle I could cover with my hand" (*T* 173)

The makeshift clan of Nanapush, Fleur, Eli, Lulu, Margaret, and Nector harvest the land of as many salable items like cranberry bark and hides as possible, which is consistent with cash-desperate Ojibwa of the reservation at this point in time (Peterson 987). They raise just enough money to pay the taxes due on their respective allotments. When Nector takes the money to town, however, he is confronted with exorbitant(and bogus) late fees, and only has enough money to save his mother's land. The lumber company swoops in to Matchimanito soon after, and Nanapush can't stop the injustice despite his best efforts with the agent:

> "How much of that good price, that illegal late fee perhaps, splashed into your pockets? How much is stored in the walls of the Lazzarres? How much cash did you stuff into the mattress of Bernadette?" (*T* 208)

Fleur and Nanapush were among the nearly 70% of Turtle Mountain members who had lost their allotments by 1920. The Kashpaws, Morrisseys, Lazzarres, and Pukwans were the fortunate minority. As we have seen, this minority was larger than the one at White Earth. It may be that the richer land and easier corruption at the latter gave the Turtle Mountain few more room to maneuver, as the biggest timber barons had zeroes in on White Earth. Matchimanito, however, was to rich a prize to pass up.

The town of Argus also figures prominently in *Tracks*. "Like its Greek counterpart, Argos, the town contains life-giving elements central to each character and his or her personality. Argos is inextricable from Jason in preindustrial Greek sacred stories, and likewise Argus is a source of identification and a repository of values that each character seeks or rejects" (Hafen 328). It also has an uncanny resemblance to Erdrich's hometown, Wahpeton. Argus is described by Pauline in 1913 as,

> "just a grid of six streets on either side of the railroad depot. There were two elevators, one central, the other a few miles west. Two stores competed for the trade of the three hundred citizens, and three churches quarreled with one another for their souls." (*T* 12-13)

In her piece "A Writer's Beginnings", the first recollections Erdrich shares of her hometown are meadowlark song and the, "giant elms that stretched down the straight streets laid out by railroad plat" (Erdrich 1). In "A Writer's Sense of Place," which predates *Tracks*, Erdrich states that, "in a tribal view of the world, where one place has been inhabited for generations, the landscape becomes enlivened by a sense of group and family history" (Erdrich 1). After a meditation on regionalist like Marquez, Faulkner, Welty, and even Cheever, Erdrich states that for her work the sense of place is influenced by where she grew up, "a small North Dakota town, on land that once belonged to the Wahpeton-Sisseton Sioux," before recounting the now-commonly known biographical details of her parents who worked at the Indian School and her grandfather who was chairman of the Turtle Mountain tribe (Erdrich 4).

There is further evidence in *Tracks* that the story is set in North Dakota. In chapter three, Nanapush reports that in 1913 and 1914, "my newspaper came from Grand Forks once a week" (*T* 47). The geographic distance between the characters and Grand Forks is further felt by Pauline in chapter four, when she states that Bernadette, "decided to send Sophie far away, to Grand Forks, where a strict aunt lived, devout and childless, next door to a church" (*T* 87). When Lulu is sent away to the government boarding school by Fleur, it was evidently south, for, "Nector chose to go south after he finished grade eight, even farther away than you, down to the state of Oklahoma" *(T* 225). One infers that the school Lulu went to is based on the Wahpeton Indian School, where both of Erdrich's parents worked when she was a child. "Constructed in the earliest decade of the last century and opened in 1908, the school was created to educate Native children from surrounding reservations—

mainly those in North Dakota, South Dakota, and Minnesota" (Erdrich 3). Erdrich's grandfather was a student there in 1915, four years prior to the start of Lulu's stay. These locales may be closer to Minnesota in the novel than in real-life, but they are not in the state: in chapter two, Pauline reports that Pete and Fritzie, employees of the butcher shop in Argus, "left for Minnesota to escape the heat" (*T* 22).

The location of *Tracks* is well stated by Julie Maristuen-Rodakowski: "the fiction of Louise Erdrich, although not set directly on the Turtle Mountain Reservation, is based solidly on the facts of that area of North Dakota and on its Native American history" (Rodakowski 40). Why is this important to a reader of *Tracks*? Consider that many Americans now have at least a vague awareness of the massacre at Wounded Knee in 1890. Though this awareness is helpful, the slaughter of the Ghost Dancers was far from the only one perpetrated against indigenous peoples by their colonizers: in fact, it was the pathetic last massacre of the last gasp of unified resistance. The excessive focus on Wounded Knee risks creating an impression in the popular imagination that it was the *only* or the *most* wanton massacre that was ever committed against indigenous people, when in fact it was far from either of these two superlatives. Likewise, a complacent linking of *Tracks* with the swindle against the White Earth Anishinaabeg marginalizes the like frauds and proto-frauds that were committed against scores of other tribes, including the one the book's author intended to portray, the Turtle Mountain Ojibwe. The abuses the characters in *Tracks* contend with were the premeditated policies of the federal government, and were directly responsible for the epidemic disease, abject poverty, and family disintegration portrayed in the novel. Likewise, in the mainstream consciousness, "Indian" history ends in 1890 with Wounded Knee and the census bureau's declaration that the frontier was closed. With *Tracks*, Erdrich picks up close to where the mainstream narrative leaves off, the period of, "transition from a subsistence society to the economic realities of modernism" (Hafen 326).

There is also a potential political subtext to efforts to place the events of *Tracks* in Minnesota that could be quite pernicious: In her piece on the White Earth travesty, Erdrich describes the contemporary governor of the state and his appointees as, "public servants whose views on Indian sovereignty put them light years ahead of their counterparts in most other states" (Dorris-Erdrich 3). The difference between present and past is less stark in the Dakotas, as epitomized by the presence of the 'militant' American Indian Movement and such polarizing political figures as William "Wild Bill" Janklow, who became the longest-serving governor in South Dakota history despite a persona of open hostility to Native interests and persistent allegations that he had raped a 15 year old Lakota girl as a young politico and evaded prosecution. Placing *Tracks* in Minnesota helps divert attention from the modern political economy of the Dakotas in favor of a 'progressive' state with seemingly more distance from its violent and racist past.

Hafen states that, "Louise Erdrich's home ground is Turtle Mountain, North Dakota. That place is inseparable from who she is" (Hafen 331). As such, her determination to reclaim Ojibwe history from its colonialist oppressors informs her historical fiction about what was likely the bleakest period the band experienced. The least a respectful reader can do is to affirm its true setting.

Works cited

Camp, Gregory S. "Working Out Their Own Salvation: The Allotment of Land in Severalty and the Turtle Mountain Chippewa Band, 1870-1920." *American Indian Culture and Research Journal*; Volume 14, Issue 2 (1990) 19-38. Print.

Erdrich, Louise. "A Writer's Beginnings." *Smithsonian*; Volume 37, Issue 5 (2006) Print.

Erdrich, Louise. *Tracks*. New York: Harper and Row, 1988. Print.

Erdrich, Louise. "Where I Ought To Be: A Writer's Sense of Place." *New York Times Book Review*; July 28, 1985, p. 1. Print.

Erdrich, Louise and Dorris, Michael. "Who Owns The Land?" *The New York Times Magazine,* September 4, 1988. Print.

Hafen, P. Jane. "'We Anishinaabeg Are the Keepers of the Names of the Earth':
Louise Erdrich's Great Plains." *Great Plains Quarterly*, Fall 2001, 321-32. Print.

Larson, Sidner. "The Fragmentation of a Tribal People in Louise Erdrich's *Tracks*."
American Indian Culture and Research Journal; Volume 17, Issue 2, (1993) 1-13.
Print.

Maristuen-Rodakowski, Julie. "The Turtle Mountain Reservation in North Dakota: It's
History as Depicted in Louise Erdrich's *Love Medicine* and *Beet Queen*."*American
Indian Culture and Research Journal;* Volume 12, Issue 3 (1988): 33-48. Print.

Meyer, Melissa L. "Dispossession and the White Earth Anishinaabeg, 1889-1920."
American Historical Review; Volume 96, Issue 2 (1991) 368-94 Print.

Peterson, Nancy J. "History, Postmodernism, and Louise Erdrich's *Tracks*." *PMLA*;
Volume 109, Issue 5 (1994) 982-994. Print.

Quennet, Fabienne C. *Where 'Indians' Fear To Tread: A Postmodern Reading of
Louise Erdrich's North Dakota Quartet*. Munster: Lit Verlag, 2000. Print.

Stookey, Lorena L. *Louise Erdrich: A Critical Companion*. Westport, CT: Greenwood
Press, 1999. Print.

Stripes, James D. "The Problem(s) of (Anishinaabe) History in the Fiction of Louise
Erdrich: Voices and Contexts." *Wicazo Sa Review;* Volume 7, Issue 2 (1991) 26-32.
Print.